A BROOKINGS ALBUM

1879-2004
Celebrating 125 Years

To Peggy &
To my much older
neighbor

Chuck Cecil

Chuck Cecil

Library of Congress Control Number: 2003094588

ISBN: 1-893490-06-8

On The cover...
This scene looks west toward Volga. It was taken from the
smoke stack of the Power Plant that was once at the corner
of Fourth Street and Fifth Avenue where the parking lot
next to the Elks Club is today. The building in the foreground was the city's first school and later became the
offices of the *Brookings Register*. The brick building at the
northeast corner of Main Avenue and Fourth Street, upper
left, the Binford Building, which once housed Kendall's
Pharmacy, is still standing and in use. This photo is be-
lieved to have been taken about the turn of the century.

Printed in the United States of America
Pine Hill Press
4000 West 57th Street
Sioux Falls, SD 57106

Introduction

This photo album of Brookings, South Dakota, captures tiny bits and pieces of the history of some-place special. It was not the intent to gather in one place a complete and representative set of photographs touching every aspect of life in Brookings for all of its 125 years. For one thing, photographs of the first five or six decades of the community are few and far between. For another, there simply aren't enough pages for a complete photographic history of our town.

My purpose was to provide brief glimpses of how it used to be. If one assumes that each photograph required a film exposure of fractions of seconds, the over 250 photographs pasted down in this album represent perhaps less than a few minutes of time out of a century and a quarter of community life.

For many of you who thumb through this album, the photos will provide a nostalgic trip back to another time and another place in your life. You may see friends or old haunts or former work places. For younger viewers, these black and whites will be an introduction to what it was like during the long, arduous process of smoothing our community's rough edges, and working each day to make it a better place. I hope you all enjoy this brief journey back in time.

Acknowledgments

The old and not so old photographs in this book, some of which were frayed and faded, came from many sources. Some were my own, received during nearly fifty years of newspapering. I have also collected old postcards and pictures of Brookings for many years. Thanks to George Norby, who has an extensive collection of Brookings photographs that were useful in the preparation of this album. The files of the Brookings County Historical Society also yielded many of the pictures selected for use. Thanks also to the Brookings Public Library, to Nathelle DeHaan, Shirley Lyons, the Town and Country Shopper, and Doris Roden and the Downtown Improvement Office.

A special thanks, too, to my wife Mary and daughter Amy Cecil Holm for publication advice and proof reading. Finally, my thanks to the others who have provided details concerning certain photographs, and for remembering addresses and names and instances related to the pictures published in this 125th Anniversary Album.

— Chuck Cecil

This book is dedicated to George Norby and his wife Evelyn, who, unfortunately, died May 8, 2002. George and Evelyn were tireless recorders of Brookings history, converting their small dining room into a document collection and storage center. They started their hobby and labor of love in 1986 after George retired as a printer for the *Brookings Register*. Each day since then, perusing newspapers and other documents, they have recorded on their computer and hard copy files the town's comings and goings.

After retiring, while working at the *Register* part-time, George was appalled to learn that the newspaper's old photographs were being thrown into the trash heap. Fortunately for us all, he rescued many of them, especially old, one-of-a-kind, irreplacable photographs. Many of these are in this album. Because of the Norbys' untiring dedication to the preservation of Brookings' past, it pleases me to dedicate this book to them. With Evelyn's passing, George continues preservation work the couple started.

George and Evelyn at work in their dining room. Note the bookcase behind them that is filled with historic documents and photographs.

Table of Contents

Happy 125th Birthday Brookings!

Looking northeast toward the SDSC campus "on the hill" in the late 1890s from atop a grain elevator. The Brookings House Hotel is at far right and the small house across Main Avenue from it is where the Masonic Temple building would be constructed. The first Brookings County Courthouse (5), a wood-frame edifice built in 1883, is at far right, above the Brookings Hotel.

Buildings on campus at this time were a large barn (1), Old North (2), Old Central (3), and the Extension Building (4). Note the outhouses behind the downtown buildings, and the absence of brick buildings. The street running from lower left to right is Third Street. George Norby Photo.

vi

Chapter One

Street Scenes

Apparently, clearing snow from Main Avenue wasn't a high priority in the 1920s, when horse power under the hood and horse power under the harness were reluctantly co-existing. Note the car at right, mired in a snow-bank, while a span of white horses and a wagon turn the corner onto Main Avenue off Front Street. Downtown Improvement Photo.

This photo was taken about 1900 looking north down Main Avenue from the railroad tracks. Notice the contraption at right, known as a railroad gate. It was lowered to stop traffic as trains passed through town. The building at right is the Brookings House Hotel, which was later damaged by fire and was closed. The next building with the tower front is the Montgomery Ward building at Third Street and Main. George Norby Photo.

In this picture taken in the early 1900s, the city had installed an overhead street light at each downtown intersection. A horse and buggy are at far left. Another team and buggy are making the turn east at the intersection of Third Street and Main. Sidewalks are of cement with cement crosswalks, but the road is dirt with a smattering of gravel and horse manure mixed in. Some progress had apparently been made since the top photograph was taken. There are more power lines and more growth on the tree which appears at left in both pictures. The Brookings Hardware Store is at far right. Brookings Public Library Photo.

Tracks visible in the dirt that is Main Avenue indicate where on this particular day, wagons and buggies dodged muddy areas. The photograph was taken in about 1895 looking south. Note the elevated sidewalks made of wood, which kept pedestrians out of the muck and mud except when it was necessary to cross from one side of Main to the other. The raised sidewalk is probably because in those days, when the Big Sioux River flooded, waters could reach to downtown Brookings. George Norby Photo.

Even in 1919, with the auto having all but replaced the horse as the accepted mode of transportation, all was not perfect on the streets and highways. This photo, looking south from Fifth Street, includes the sign in the foreground admonishing drivers to "keep right." Parking was a matter of choice. Some parked diagonally, at left, or parallel, at right. The peaked tower in the background is the Masonic Temple, built in 1894 and still standing today, without the tower. George Norby Photo.

Advances in technology usually exceeded the city's ability to respond with laws and policies. That is certainly evident in this 1930s Main Avenue picture. Parking seems to be helter skelter, especially for those having to park in the center lane. The city finally addressed the problem after an accident that injured a farm woman who was in town for Saturday shopping. A single row of cars was, for a time, allowed to park diagonally, but that was soon abandoned and center parking was forever outlawed. George Norby Photo.

Mid-morning traffic on Main Avenue in the late 1980s. The middle lane is now assigned as a turning lane. Note the false front, since removed, on the Montgomery Ward Building at right. Photograph looks north. Chuck Cecil Photo.

This generously embellished map shows Brookings at the age of one year. The artist took some liberties. The tree-lined square at the top is intended to represent the college, but it is in the wrong location. At the time, streets were named after prominent local individuals and the city's avenues were named after states. Eighth Avenue, for example, was at that time Minnesota Avenue.

This scene looks out from the courthouse roof northwest toward the Post Office, clearly visible in the center. George Norby Photo.

Parking meters were for leaning on, too, as shown in the opposite-page photo of the east side of Main Avenue between Fifth and Fourth Streets in the 1950s. Above, Nickburgers were selling for 15 cents each and motorists braved a 1963 blizzard-built snowdrift to buy them. George Norby Photo.

Looking south on the west side of Main Avenue following a 1975 blizzard. The now-closed Coast to Coast store had the only overhanging awning in town. Owner Harry Jones has since closed and has converted the store into an office complex. George Norby Photo.

The Allison home at Third Street and Sixth Avenue, now the location of the Brookings Public Library. The Allisons were prominent residents and owners of considerable land surrounding Brookings, as well as owners of a successful land office on Main Avenue. Brookings Public Library Photo.

This neo-classic revival style home was built over a period of two years by Horace Fishback, Sr. and completed in 1902. Since then, it has been the continuous home of members of the Fishback family. Its current residents are Van and Barbara Fishback. The three-story home has 7,553 square feet of space and 14 rooms. Ceilings in most of the lower-level rooms have intricate stenciled designs. The unique dining room is oval-shaped with oval floor-to-ceiling windows looking out on an enclosed east-side porch. The original intercom system connects the upstairs master bedroom with the kitchen below. Behind the home is the carriage and livestock barn which was completed about a year before the home. Three carriages and a sleigh are still stored in the barn. Chuck Cecil Photo.

Looking west on Fourth Street from the water tower between Eleventh and Twelfth Avenue. The Catholic Church with its original tower is one block away. The tower was later removed. A new church was built at the site in the 1950s and is now a commercial establishment. The white house at far left along the alley behind the church still stands. Below, two girls hurry past the city Telephone Office, also on Fourth Street. The department has expanded along the entire half block. George Norby Photos.

Otto Arneson stands in the door of his blacksmith and buggy shop at 144 South Main Avenue. Next door, Mrs. Hanna Arneson is standing next to Mr. and Mrs. Palmer and their two daughters. The shop was later owned by Bill Mitz, then Harry Kellogg, then George Cubbage, and then Harvey Hai. George Norby Photo.

A blizzard in 1963 during the Christmas season brought traffic to a standstill. This picture looks south at the Fourth Street and Main intersection. George Norby Photo.

In 1952, one of the homes featured in *Better Homes and Gardens* magazine was this ranch style at 817 Eighth Street. It was built by Mr. and Mrs. Russell D. Cole, who at the time were owners of Cole's Department Store. Chuck Cecil Photo.

This house in the Prairie School design at the corner of Main Avenue and Eighth Street was built in 1920 by Ivan Cobel, who was the cashier at the First National Bank. It cost $22,000 and was the most expensive built in 1920. Exterior features include thick battered piers and porch columns, exposed purlins and rafters, and the cladding combination of clapboard, brick, and concrete. Owners Jim and Doris Roden have refurbished the interior while keeping its original style and design. Chuck Cecil Photo.

Chapter Two

University Scenes

Solberg Hall on campus is the oldest building still in use. Its interior was recently torn out and competely rebuilt. It was originally the Engineering Building and is again being used by the College of Engineering. SDSU Photo.

Crowds gather on the campus green about 1900 for a military review. Old North (also pictured below), the Pharmacy Building (Chemistry), and Old Central are shown in the background. The military program, always a part of SDSU, early on earned the school the title "West Point of the Plains."

George Norby Photos.

The Horticulture Building is the oldest building in its original condition now on the campus. (Solberg Hall, the oldest, was remodeled in 2002-03 for $3.9 million in gifts to the SDSU Foundation.) The Horticulture Building, originally the Plant Breeding Building, was completed in 1901 a few months after Solberg Hall. SDSU Photo.

The animal husbandry barn in its day was the most elaborate barn in the state. Note the ramp and bridge to the barn's second floor. Electric lighting came to the campus in 1896, and this made the barn even more spectacular. It was located where the H. M. Briggs Library is now located. SDSU Photo.

The start of each quarter was hectic on campus. These mid-1950s students crowded into the tiny Pugsley Student Union bookstore built in the early 1940s. The bookstore was in this small space until a new Union was built in 1973 for $2.8 million. By 2003, that facility was too small and a plan was developed to enlarge it for a student body in excess of 10,000. SDSU Photo.

Chances are that the students shown in the top photo headed for this building and its famous ice cream cones after their book buying trip was over. For years, over a small counter in this Dairy Science Building, as it appears here in 1916, passed the famous overflowing cones available in many flavors. The water tower at right, north of "The Barn" (gymnasium), was no longer needed and was cut down in 1956. George Norby Photo.

As an adjunct to the College of Pharmacy greenhouse that was built onto the south end of the Administration Building, as shown in this pre-1941 photo, a sunken garden was constructed in which to grow acquatic plants having medicinal value. It was known as the Japanese Garden. After the start of WW II with Japan, students drained the garden, filled it in and planted grass. The garden remains buried today, although during a hot, dry month, its outline can still be seen. George Norby Photo.

When WW II ended, young men and women returned home, married, and enrolled in college. SDSU met the need for married students by hauling surplus barracks from army posts and Corps of Engineers Missouri River dam projects. In all, enough barracks for 108 apartments and fifty trailer houses were brought to the campus and placed where the current Student Union stands. The area was known as "Fertile Acres." George Norby Photo.

Lawrence DeHaan came to SDSC from Platte in the early 1930s to pursue a degree in what was then Animal Husbandry. He graduated in 1937, and after a career with the Bureau of Indian Affairs, retired and returned with his wife to live in Brookings. Here DeHaan is leading a horse into the Stock Pavilion, which was built in 1918. It has since been converted into the Agricultural Heritage Museum. Nathelle DeHaan Photo.

With the completion of the Coughlin Campanile in 1929, photographers could record campus scenes from a new perspective. A graveled Medary Avenue carries traffic past Woodbine Cottage, Wecota and Winona Halls, and the Stock Pavilion (shown above). Woodbine was built by President Lewis McLouth as his residence. He served a tumultuous nine years, from 1887 to 1896, and left amidst controversy. Before departing, he gave Woodbine to the University. The cottage has been home to every president since. George Norby Photo.

The Pride of the Dakotas Marching Band, directed by Jim McKinney, has been in demand to perform for professional football game halftime shows, presidential inaugural parades, and in 2003, the Rose Bowl parade. The 2003 band of 350 was the largest ever at SDSU. SDSU Photo Montage.

Solberg Hall was built in 1901 and served as the school's engineering building for many years. In deteriorating condition, it was condemned in 1998. In 2002-03, using gifts to the SDSU Foundation, its interior was gutted and reconstructed. Some of the scrap lumber was rescued by Conrad Solberg, above, a 1958 engineering graduate from White Bear Lake, MN, who built a conference room table from the wood in memory of his uncle, Halvor Solberg, after whom the building was named.

In 2000, work started on the refurbishing of Coughlin Campanile, built in 1929. In addition to tuck pointing and repair of exterior facings, crews on the $550,000 project also removed nearly an 80-year accumulation of pigeon droppings, which amounted to over five cubic yards. Chuck Cecil Photos.

The South Dakota Art Museum was completed in 1970 at a cost of $500,000 from alumni and friends. It was the building at left. An addition was recently added, greatly expanding display and storage space. Chuck Cecil Photo.

A dairy student and friend, probably taken in the 1930s.

Except for the most obvious routes between buildings, sidewalks are never built on the SDSU campus until it is determined by student use where the walks should be. Most student-made paths have been covered in this 1980s campus view. Behind the Rotunda is the Nursing/Family and Consumer Sciences/Arts and Sciences Building, originally dubbed the "Hen House" (Home Economics/Nursing). In the upper left corner is part of the ROTC building, built during the 1930s as a WPA project. At upper right is the Student Union Building, which will be expanded soon. The residence hall at right center is Mathews Hall. SDSU Photo.

Sherwood O. Berg, who in 1970 would become the first SDSU alumnus to serve as the President of South Dakota State University, is shown here during basic training as a ROTC cadet in WW II. He was a member of the 44 Kings, so named because after being commissioned, the SDSU contingent returned to campus to await assignment. Berg would fight in Europe as a mortar platoon commander. Before being named SDSU's president, he was dean of the College of Agriculture at the University of Minnesota.
Sherwood Berg Photo.

22

In the early 1900s, a fall tradition at State College was the annual Bag Rush, which pitted sophomore men against freshmen. Three large bags filled with rags were lined up on the football field's 50-yard line. The winning class was the team that pushed the most bags over their goal line in the half-hour contest. Rules prevented slugging and punching, but other than that it was a raucous free-for-all that delighted spectators and partcipants alike. A 1912 *Industrial Collegian* story mentioned that each bag weighed 500 pounds, but it was written in a humorous vein and the truth might have been somewhat embellished. After the event, a celebratory picnic was held on the campus green. SDSU Photo.

A Hobo Day pep rally probably about 1915, decades before the term "political correctness" was invented. Hobo Day was started in 1912 and has continued since. In the early years, men dressed as hoboes and co-eds as Native American women. The camera is looking toward Woodbine Cottage, the president's home, in the background at right center. SDSU Photo.

In recent years, SDSU has computerized its registration process, but it was still business as usual in 1992 with an antiquated process that created long lines, short tempers, and considerable frustration. Brookings Register Photo.

The most violent Hobo Day in history took place Oct. 22, 1990. Hundreds of students went on a rampage on campus and in the Brookings community, causing tens of thousands of dollars in damages. Many were apprehended and some served jail time. One ring-leader spent nearly a year in the county jail. Since this episode, Hobo Day has returned to its usual boisterous but sane homecoming. Brookings Register Photo.

Chapter Three

People

Hank Claussen, Elkton farmer, was one of the county's most popular and recognizable politicians. In his ever-present trademark tub-sized hat, which is now in the Brookings County History Museum inVolga, Hank served a total of 18 years as County Sheriff. He was first elected in 1935, served on and off as the law governing sheriff's terms allowed, and died of a heart attack while on duty in 1955. Brookings Register Photo.

A group, including Civil War veterans in the front row wearing their service caps, poses in front of the Farmers and Merchants Bank, built in 1903 at 314 and 316 Main Avenue where Langland's is today. In later years, Jesse Cutler had a radio and ice cream shop in the building, which was torn down in 1952. George Norby Photo.

Long-time Brookings Depot Agent Howard Graham, right, and Mayor Homer Dwiggins exchange greetings at the corner of Fourth Street and Main Avenue in 1951. Graham had a 40-year career with North Western Railroad and served in Brookings from 1935 to 1952. Dwiggins was first elected mayor in 1939, serving until 1952. He was elected again in 1954 and served until 1960. Shirley Lyons Photo.

Johnny Mix, left, and Ferdie Rausch in front of Mix Market in 1952. The poster in the window is a "Welcome Ike" sign. Dwight Eisenhower visited Brookings on a campaign swing through South Dakota that year. George Norby Photo.

Gus Bowers, in hat, and KBRK radio salesman Wally Stangland during Crazy Days in 1961. Bowers, who came to America from Greece, owned and operated B&G Billiards at 421 Main, where the Safari Lounge is today. Town & Country Shopper photo.

The Brookings Police Department staff in the late 1950s, from left, Norman (Slim) Gilbert, Orville Overski, Police Chief J. J. Connelly, Bob Schuld, and Emil Hansen. George Norby Photo.

Members of the Board of Directors of the Farmers Cooperative in Brookings in 1934 were, front row from left, Guy Derdall, Oscar Wetterstad, Manager Alfred Jermstad and Ted LeFevre. Back row from left, John Johnston, Albert Oines, Oscar Hanson, Gus Hutchendorf, Carl Trygstad, unknown, and a Mr. Gamble. Brookings Public Library Photo.

Cutting it up during the 1961 Crazy Days celebration are two unrecognizables at left, then *Brookings Register* Publisher Art Mitchell in center, auto dealers Gene Kjellsen and Larry Frie, far right. Below, a band of Brookings High school musicians entertained. Town & Country Shopper Photos.

Animal Control Warden Earl Hammer in the early 1950s. On the 1951 Personal Property Tax reporting forms, Brookings residents who claimed ownership of dogs numbered 321. Interestingly, the city auditor reported that year that only 32 dogs were properly licensed by the city. George Norby Photo.

In the 1950s, Monty Harming was one of the last of the early-morning risers, delivering Bibby-Kallemeyn (BK) grade A dairy products to Brookings homes. In this photo, his rack is filled with chocolate milk in front, regular milk behind and some cottage cheese in a convenient holder on top. George Norby Photo.

In 1964, Chief J. J. Connelly, right, passed the badge to Doug Filholm. In 1969 Filholm hired the first female patrol officer, Lillian Boswell. Below, veteran radioman Bert Getz and businessman and later mayor Orrin Juel work the airwaves at KBRK during the 1961 Crazy Days. Town & Country Shopper Photo.

The staff dressed down at Quail's Clothing, located in the building now next to The Ram, for the 1961 Crazy Days celebration. From left are Buck Connelley, Bob Norton, Cal Quail and unidentified. Town & Country Shopper Photo.

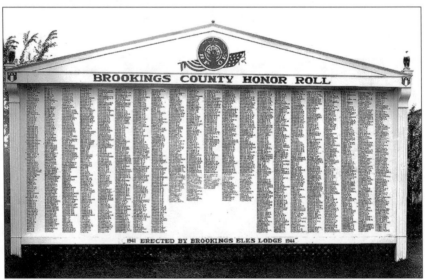

Under sponsorship of the Elks Club, a large honor roll board was erected just south of the City Armory during ceremonies in 1944. More than 2,000 servicemen and women were listed. It fell into disrepair after WW II and was taken down in 1951. David Mitchell Photo.

College Sociology Professor Douglas Chittick, who later served on the City Commission, helped at the Kiwanis Club booth at the 1961 Crazy Days celebration. Chittick Gardens is named in his honor. Town & Country Shopper Photo.

Gip Nolan, Chamber of Commerce executive, at his office on Main, where the Wells Fargo Bank's parking lot is now. In the 1950s, the Chamber earned extra money as the Western Union office. George Norby Photo.

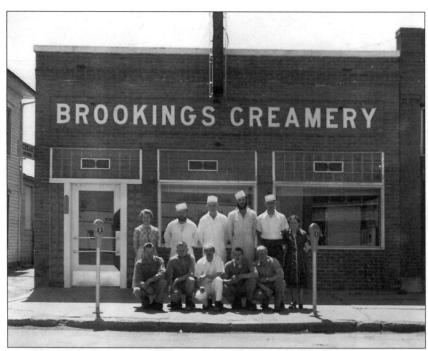

The staff at the Brookings Creamery in 1951. The creamery was at 422 Fourth Street. George Norby Photo.

Harold's Plumbing and Heating at 410 Fifth Street in 1954. Owner Harold Halstead is at left. George Norby Photo.

Brookings Auctioneers Ray Barnett, left, and Bob Peterson, at work in the 1950s. Peterson continues to call sales and is the oldest practicing auctioneer in the state. George Norby Photo.

Harold Niklason started Nick's Hamburger Shop in 1929, selling his sandwiches for five cents each. The little shop on the corner remains a popular eating spot today.
H. Niklason, Jr. photo.

"Buy 'em by the sack full"

•○ ARNOLD *"nig"* JOHNSON ○•

THE PRIDE OF BROOKINGS —

A 147-POUND PACKAGE OF DYNAMITE AT QUARTERBACK. NIG RUNS, PASSES, PUNTS, CALLS THE SIGNALS and GOES ALL THE WAY ON DEFENSE

NIG'S GENERALSHIP and STEADY PLAY LED BROOKINGS TO A 19-1 CAGE RECORD

HE WAS NAMED TO THE ALL-STATE "A" TEAM AS A SOPHOMORE, JUNIOR, and SENIOR.

HE LED BROOKINGS TO A TIE FOR THE 1952 ESD TITLE and BRILLIANTLY ENGINEERED A 14-14 TIE WITH SIOUX FALLS

SODAK SPORTS "ATHLETE OF THE YEAR"

NIG WILL BE GRADUATED THIS SPRING AS A 12 LETTERMAN — 4 IN FOOTBALL, 4, IN BASKETBALL, and 4 IN TRACK ; AND, HIS COACHES FIGURE BASEBALL IS HIS LONG SUIT.

BROAD JUMPING IS HIS SPECIALTY. HE LEAPED 20'-4¼" IN THE MUD AT THE ABERDEEN RELAYS and HAS HIS SIGHTS SET ON THE STATE TITLE.

He was perhaps the greatest all-round athlete ever in Brookings, graduating from BHS in 1953 with 12 letters, four each in football, basketball and track. Arnold Johnson's nickname was also his father's, who coached at BHS. Arnold was named to the all-state basketball team three years in a row.

Kid Hartwick, as assistant wrestling coach for the SDSC wrestling team in the 1920s.

Members of the Chamber of Commerce Board of Directors in 1949. Back row from left, Floyd Poole, Harold Urevig, Tom Hart, Charlie Poole and Vernon Rude. Seated, Irving Brown, William (Gip) Nolan, chamber executive; Herb Cheever, Jim Bane, and Howard Graham. Shirley Lyons Photo.

When the historic first annual Beef Bowl game was held at South Dakota State University in the fall of 1967, senior Carol Bagby, front, of Rapid City became the school's first Beef Bowl Queen. Her court included from left Patty Marshall, also of Rapid City; Barb Hageman of Redfield; Pam Rothbauer, Sioux Falls; and Twyla Conkey of Miller. The Beef Bowl was the brainchild of Stan Marshall, who was athletic director at SDSU at the time. Incidentally, SDSU didn't fare well in that first Beef Bowl game, losing to powerhouse North Dakota State University by a score of 34-14. That season, Coach Ralph Ginn's Jackrabbits had four wins and six loses. SDSU Photo.

This beer joint, the Seven-O Club (its telephone number) was in the same building as Nick's Hamburger Shop in 1944. It's now a barber shop.The top photo is of some of the '44 Kings, celebrating the wedding of ROTC member Tom Lyons and Shirley Graham of Brookings on Oct. 8, 1943. All of the men served in WW II. One, Gil Ambur at far right, was killed in action eleven months later, on Sept. 15, 1944. Below, another group of collegiates with owner Jim Urquhart, probably in the same year because the Sturdevant Auto calendar on the wall has the same picture. The place had standing room only at the bar plus elevated plank seats behind it. Note the softball schedule on the blackboad in picture below. Future Brookings business-man Gene Waltz is second from right, below. George Norby and Shirley Lyons Photos.

Brookings businessman and Korean War veteran Harry Jones had an idea in late 1980. By the early 1990s he was busy working with veterans' groups and Brookings and county governmental entities to raise the funds and in-kind services to construct a fitting memorial to all county veterans. The result of an intensive fund drive provided resources to build the memorial which is now located in west Brookings adjacent to the Highway 14 bypass near the former location of Frie Motors. The memorial salutes veterans of every branch of service.

Brookings Register Photo.

Popular Brookings attorney George S. Mickelson was elected to a second term as governor on Nov. 6, 1990, defeating Democrat Bob Samuelson. Mickelson's father had served as governor. Brookings Register Photo.

On April 19, 1993, returning from an industrial development trip to Ohio, Governor George S. Mickelson and seven others died when the state plane crashed while trying to land at the Dubuque, Iowa, airport after the craft experienced engine trouble. This was the crash scene on the Rose Marie Ambrosy's farm near Dubuque. Brookings Register/Associated Press Photo.

Orville Duff was a person most people who did business in Brookings over a 70-year period knew. Orville was still at work six days a week at his tire shop at 319 Third Street on June 15, 1992, his 90th birthday, when this photo was taken of him by *Register* photographer at the time, Eric Landwehr. Duff opened his shop in the late 1920s and prided himself in hot patching inner tubes, instead of the more modern cold patches. One lightbulb provided light in his nondescript shop, and he heated the place with a dependable old wood stove, burning both wood scraps he picked up in the community, and discarded cardboard boxes and papers he found in the streets and alleys of downtown Brookings. He said he was able to work well past the usual retirement age because he never smoked or drank and he exercised regularly. Orville was the dean of Brookings businessmen until his death a few years after this photo was taken. Brookings Register Photo.

Chapter Four

Business and Commerce

Gathering on a Sunday afternoon, sales personnel and clients of the Allison Land Office, all dressed to the nines, pose at the southeast intersection of Third Street and Main Avenue. In the early years, Allison employees assisted settlers in locating claims, and sold thousands of abandoned claims. Note the elaborate intersection lighting system curving out over the street, with electric lights every few feet. Brookings Public Library Photo.

John S. Roberts and P. W. Waltz were partners in 1920 in a hardware business that was eventually operated by Waltz and his sons Gene and Rex, at 406 Main Avenue. Gene Waltz assumed full ownership in 1960. This photo was taken in the 1950s. George Norby Photo.

This crude contraption is a well-drilling rig in front of the Brookings House Hotel, which was located across the street east from the present-day City Auditorium. What became known as the Montgomery Ward Building is in the background. George Norby Photo.

A popular "watering hole" for collegiates in the 1950s and 60s was B&G Billiards, located at 421 Main Avenue. It was operated by Gus Bowers who emigrated from Greece. He was generous in lending money to cash-strapped college men, holding watches or rings as collateral. After a few years, he had several cigar boxes filled with unclaimed jewelry. George Norby Photo.

"Filling Up Over The Years"

A "fill-up" in the teens came with real horse power. Ted Fliesner's Texaco and others were later established. And since 1929, Brookings residents have stopped by Nick's Hamburger Shop to fill up on a sack full of Nick's famous "gut-bombs." The picture of Fliesner's station was taken in about 1954. George Norby Photos (right and center); Brookings Register Photo (bottom).

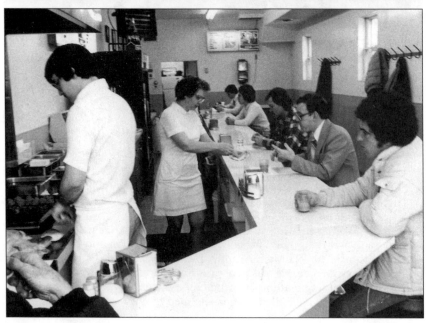

The office staff and elevator workers gathered in the austere Farmers Cooperative business office in May 1919. Note the electrical wire fastened to the window frame and the office's one overhead light. Brookings Public Library Photo.

In 1945, an enterprising Brookings High School vocational-agricultural instructor, Wilmer Davis, had the idea that hybrid seed corn would be in great demand as the nation got back on its economic feet following WW II. He spearheaded the effort to establish Sokota certified seeds. The business first opened in this old abandoned ice house on First Street, a block east of Main Avenue. It later established a two square-block complex on Second Street South. The business was sold to a national firm in 1985. George Norby Photo.

The city's first hotel, the Brookings House, was opened in December 1879 on Main Avenue, across the street east of the present City Auditorium. Sherman Poole operated the hotel for a number of years. This picture was taken in 1885. On March 19, 1910, a kitchen fire badly damaged the hotel. A city ordinance at the time prohibited repair of wooden structures if fire damaged more than 50 percent of the building, so the hotel was not repaired. George Norby Photo.

In 1916, a block and one-half east of the site of the old Brookings House Hotel, Fred Cole and George Cabel purchased an existing department store on the west side of Main Avenue. In the early years, Cole's included a grocery store, which was sold in 1938 to Lyman Vining. Cole's Store eventually occupied a modern building on the east side. It was designed by Sioux Falls architect Harold Spitznagel and completed in 1938. Pauline and Russell Cole operated the store until 1973 when it was sold to Darrell Weiland. In 1983, it was purchased by Richard and Janet Brandsma, who operated it until they decided to retire in 2001. George Norby Photo.

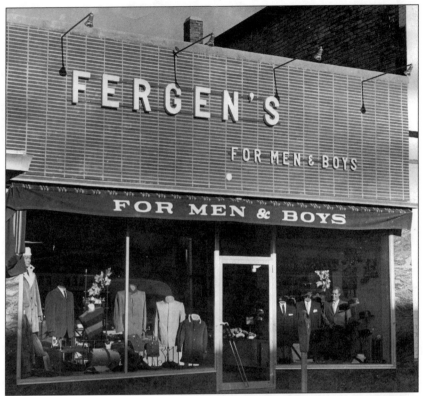

Former SDSC basketball star Jim Fergen opened his popular men's and boy's clothing store in the early 1950s. It was later purchased by John Bibby. Bibby sold the store to Ken Haug, who later sold it to present owner Steve Kirkey in 2001. Fergen's is now located across the street in the 400 block on Main Avenue. George Norby Photo.

The location of these small storage sheds along the railroad track is unknown, but they were possibly sited east of the old train depot. The horse-drawn buggies are headed north on Main Avenue. It was a busy time for the railroad and for Brookings. A new building is under construction in the background. George Norby Photo.

For many years Great Plains Supply was located at 101 Main Avenue across the railroad tracks on the west side of the street. It was later purchased by the Farmers Coop as property protection after rumors that a fast food outlet was considering the site. Len Santema moved his insurance business to the building in about 1973, first renting from the Farmers Coop before purchasing the property. George Norby Photo.

This photo of Sunshine State Hatchery at 411 Front Street was taken in 1964. George Norby Photo.

This unique building, which obviously became known as the Windmill Station, was at First Avenue and Sixth Street West. This picture was taken in 1952. Lettering on the windmill blades indicates it was at that time Frazer Motors. The sign indicates that auto glass would be installed "while you wait." For an earlier scene, see page 64. When it was torn down, the top portion of the windmill was retired to the back yard of the late Paul Prussman. It deteriorated and was finally trashed. George Norby Photo.

The winter of 1959 was a good time for Lovre Motors at 308 Sixth Street to show off its mechanized snow removal equipment. The Lovre motto, as displayed in the background, was "It's Easy To Deal With Lovre's." George Norby Photo.

Swenson Plumbing and Heating utilized a WW II quonset for its headquarters on South Main Avenue in the 1950s. The building, with a new entry, still stands north of the Barrel Drive-In at 709 South Main Avenue. It is now Ohm's Tyler Appliance owned by Kevin Ohm. George Norby Photo.

J. O. Peterson, right, was in the jewelry business in Brookings for 40 years, and in 1927, his son-in-law G. J. Fahey joined him as a partner in the Fahey-Peterson Jewelry Store. Fahey also served for a time as the night agent at the North Western Railroad Depot. George Norby Photo.

Canned goods dominated the selections at the Bee Hive General Merchandise Store established in 1904 by Andrew and Norman Olson. Sausage is stacked on the store counter and packaged garden seeds are displayed at right. The store sold everything from tinware and groceries to clothing. George Norby Photo.

Grocery stores had changed by the 1950s. Spies Super Valu, headquartered in Watertown, opened the first "super-sized" store in Brookings in the former Bozied Hatchery building at 417 Third Street. The covered parking area was somewhat unique in the 1950s. George Norby Photo.

The Montgomery Ward Building was constructed at Third Street and Main Avenue in the 1930s. The lower level is now Skinner's Bar. The cafe at left is Cook's Cafe owned by Randy Franklin. In the photo below, taken early in the 1900s, the site of the Montgomery Ward building is where the light-colored building is located at far left. George Norby Photo.

This photograph was taken from the top of the city's power plant smoke stack, then located on what is now the parking lot west of the Elks Club on Fourth Street. This scene looks west toward Main Avenue. The north-south street is Fifth Avenue. At the intersection is what was once Brookings' first school and later the home of the *Brookings Register*. Note the windmill in lower center. This photo is used courtesy of City Hall where the larger, original photograph is displayed in the basement meeting room. Brookings City Hall Photo.

Forrest Frie, who later served as Brookings' mayor, started Frie Motor Company at 410 West Sixth Street, about where West Sixth Street curves to become the Highway 14 bypass. The cafe at left is the original White Spot opened by Frie in 1948. Later, Frie built the modern dealership buildings to the right of the cafe and station. This White Spot was closed and another later opened up across the highway. George Norby Photo.

Frie Motor Company after the White Spot, located at left in the top photo, was moved to its present location across the street. (See chapter 13.) That's owner Forrest Frie standing at far right. Later, Running's Farm and Fleet moved into these buildings before locating for a time on South Main. Sandy Frie Photo.

The Sawnee Hotel was the home away from home for travelers before the big motels came to town. Its Cactus Grill served not only guests, but noon lunches for service clubs that met in the hotel's meeting room. The city's first liquor store, a tiny nook, was located at the back of the hotel. Bill Alexander owned and operated the hotel for many years. George Norby Photo.

The Arneson Store and Cafe. Note the variety of cigars in the cabinet at right. That's Will Pierce with the moustache, standing beside owner Nels Arneson. The silver coffee maker behind Arneson isn't much different than some you find today in small town cafes. The overhead light is gas-powered. George Norby Photo.

The decision in the late 1960s to locate the 3-M Medical Products Plant in Brookings was the bellwether that sparked numerous spin-off industries and other manufacturing entities to locate in Brookings. The plant required two years to build and was opened in 1971. Several additions have been made since opening day so that employee numbers have increased from the original 150 to many times that. Chuck Cecil Photo.

What a difference forty or fifty years make. It's the same corner of the Binford Block, and the same building, but in different times. Note the hitching posts behind the old car. Also, the fire hydrant out in the street seems badly placed. The drinking fountain at the Fourth Street and Main Avenue corner is more ornate than the one in front of Kendall's Drug Store below. For several years, a hospital-clinic was located upstairs. C. D. Kendall bought the store in 1903, and in 1937, his son Robert became his partner. The S&L Store can be seen in the photo below, next to Waltz Hardware Store. George Norby Photos.

The Buckingham Cafe at 310 Main Avenue in 1902. Note the wheeled baby carriage at the back. What appear to be silver coffee cups line the front of the counter. The cafe has converted from gas light to electric light, but just in case, the gas pipes remain in place. George Norby Photo.

The historic Bates Hotel gradually fell into disrepair, and in 1962, it was razed and became the site of the new Fire/Police Department building, with some of the land dedicated to the new City Hall.

Quail's Clothing was started in 1909 by C. O. Quail. In 1926 he built a new store on Main Avenue, and later, his son Cal became a partner. Cal continued to operate the business until 1968 when it was sold and became Wilson Clothing Store. George Norby Photos.

The Farmers Cooperative is still located at this site, where in the early years, farmers lined up to unload potatoes. Note the fire hydrant in foreground. In addition to handling produce and grains, the cooperative also dealt in farm machinery. Four flour mills were kept busy in the county between 1883 and 1910. George Norby Photo.

The late Guy Mayland loads milk for a winter's trip to the creamery in Brookings in the late 1940s. His farm was on land where the Brookings Hospital is now. Up to the 1940s, there were five creameries in the county, two in Brookings and one each in Volga, Elkton and White. Nathelle DeHaan Photo.

The building for George Rude's McCormick Agricultural Implements and Studebaker Wagon business in the center was built in Fountain and then moved three times, finally placed on Fourth Street in Brookings. The moves were probably made as the railroad settled on a final route through the county. The old Fountain building was later torn down to make room for The Fad theater and the Corner Grocery Store. Brookings Public Library Photo.

These are probably George Rude's McCormick harvesting machinery and some of his salesmen gathered at the A. B. Allison farm home near Brookings about 1900. It must have been a hot, late summer day because the attic windows in the home have been removed to allow air movement. According to an early Rude Implement advertisement in the local paper, the firm sold binders, mowers, rakes, grinders, Van Brant drills and seeders, Nichols and Shepard threshers, Russell threshers, road graders, and Wind stackers.
Brookings Public Library Photo.

New Massey-Harris farm equipment is displayed at Kellogg Implement at 303 Third Street in 1958. One of the window signs in the background advertises Brookings Ready Mix Concrete. George Norby Photo.

Allis Chalmers tractors at Osvog's Implement on south Highway 77 in 1964. Note the small tractor in foreground. George Norby Photo.

George Sexauer started a roller mill in Brookings in 1897 and continued to expand service to make the Sexauer Elevator Company among the nation's finest. At one time the company had 43 facilities in South Dakota, Minnesota, North Dakota, and Nebraska. Seed was sent throughout the nation and the world. The business was sold in the late 1990s. Brookings Public Library Photo.

Smoothing out the ruts and potholes in the Brookings Livestock Market's parking lot on south Main Avenue. George Norby Photo.

Jim's Feed Store in 1958 at 140 South Main Avenue. George Norby Photo.

Sheep day at the Brookings Livestock Market on South Main Avenue. Burdette Sheldon is in the ring directly in front of the auctioneer and clerk's counter. George Norby Photo.

The crew at Sexauer's Roller Mill posing in the early days with bags of their Perfection Flour. At one time, there were four flour mills in the county. George Norby Photo.

Matson Drugs at Main Avenue and Fourth Street. Below, The Sports Center, on Fifth Street where the First National Bank west parking lot is now located. Al Arndt and Warren Evans started the six-bowling lane Sports Center after WW II. Work progresses on the new First National Bank building, at left. For a few years, a portion of the Sports Center building was Horatio's, a busy pub catering to college students. George Norby Photos.

This is how Ray's Corner, originally Logue's Corner, looked in the 1950s. Tobacco and magazines were sold at the front of the store and a bar was located in the rear. Ray Schultz is behind the counter. Note the magazine rack at left. During remodeling in the 1990s, because of the narrowness of the business, the bars were picked up and carried out into the street, turned around and sited so that the back of the bar is now where the magazine rack was. Ray's Corner Photo.

When the threshing season started each fall, business came to a near standstill at Logue's Corner and everywhere in Brookings as crews spent long, hard days in the fields working with horses and dirty, dusty threshing machines of the day. Once the crops were in, farmers had money to spend on busy Saturday nights up and down Main Avenue. Brookings County Historical Society Photo.

The "windmill" in about the 1920s when it was a concession, selling cold pop and candy from the window. Carlsen's, next door at the corner of First Avenue and Sixth Street, opened as a cabinet shop, but the owner soon switched to automobile mechanics. The "drive in" sign over his door doesn't indicate it was a drive-in such as would come to Brookings in the late 1940s, but instructions to motorists wishing car work. Downtown Improvement, Doris Roden, Photo.

The Brookings Steam Laundry crew in 1921. The business, owned by Edwin C. Brownson, above, was on Fourth Street across from where the city telephone office (Swiftel) is today. Ed Fuller, Brownson's grandson, took over the business. His mother, Florence Brownson, is second from left. Ed Fuller photo.

Chapter Five

Government

Brookings lights shined brightly for the 1964 Christmas season. Brookings turned on its first fluorescent street lights at exactly 9:40 p.m. on Aug. 15, 1954. Three years later, the conversion to this new lighting was completed, and Brookings became the first city in America to be lighted the fluorescent way. George Norby Photo.

The K&P Car Clinic on Fourth Street as it appeared in the 1950s, was later sold and remodeled and is now a part of an expanded Brookings telephone department. An older section of the telephone department is at left. George Norby Photo.

Patrolman Vern Early mans the first bulky traffic radar machine in Brookings. Police officers now use hand-held radar guns which are less cumbersome than this machine, powered by an automobile battery located below the tripod. Police Department Photo.

This first city hall was constructed in 1912 at a cost of $23,000. It included city offices on the first floor, a two-bay fire hall, and upstairs space for use by the city's Commercial Club. A working clock for the roof was determined to cost too much, so the city purchased a fake clock which always showed the time as 8:17. In 1983, Paul Prussman purchased the vacated building at auction for $36,000, which was $9,000 above the appraised value. Under new ownership, it is now being refurbished. George Norby Photo.

After discussions lasting more than two decades, city leaders finally agreed in the early 1980s to build this new city hall attached to the Fire/Police Building at a cost of $685,000. Before the decision, various locations for the building were considered, including one site on Twenty-Second Avenue in east Brookings. Chuck Cecil Photo.

John Moberg operates the city's 1950s mosquito fogging machine which worked the streets and alleys in the early evening in an effort to control the pests. The city later assumed a more proactive role, seeking out breeding grounds early in the spring, and encouraging residents to clear trash and debris conducive to mosquito survival. George Norby Photo.

The fog of overly enthusiastic promotors was evident as some city leaders and others encouraged the citizens to build a large facility for livestock shows, 4-H Achievement Days and other events. Talk of a need for a building of some type for livestock shows and other agricultural events started in 1971 when it was suggested the city or county invest $500,000 for a bare-bones facility at the County Extension Office. The project grew and by the mid-1990s was on its way after a bond issue vote. The building was poorly planned and designed and underfunded. But gradually, the MultiPlex, now the Swiftel Center, was improved with added funding from the City. It has become a showcase as an excellent facility receiving increased use each year. The most recent addition was a portable basketball court. While an exact expense figure is not known, it is estimated to have cost about $12 or $13 million. Chuck Cecil Photo.

After a new fire hall was built, the city set out to replace its aging fleet of fire trucks and other emergency vehicles. In this photograph, the department displayed everything from a surplus WW II Jeep, second from right, to what has become an antique truck, fourth from right. The new fire hall was constructed on the site of the old Bates Hotel. George Norby Photo.

Under good leadership and with dedicated volunteer fire fighters, the Brookings Fire Department today continues the tradition of excellence for which the department has been known for decades. The city has invested considerable funds to upgrade the fleet and to build another smaller fire hall on East Sixth Street. The department has full-time leadership, but the other fire fighters all serve with pride on a volunteer basis. 2002 Melby Portraiture Photo.

In 1907, the city assumed responsiblity for a public hospital after private efforts failed. This 21-bed hospital was built near the SDSU campus on Harvey Dunn Street. Later, the city added on to this first building. The finished building served the city until the early 1960s. After a new city-county effort built the new hospital on Twenty-Second Avenue, the city toyed with using the vacated building for utility department functions. This failed to gain council approval and the building stood empty until the state offered to buy it for $75,000. It is now part of the campus physical plant, used as an office complex and Student Health Center. George Norby Photo.

This is the present Brookings Hospital built with help from the county. It was completed in 1964 and has been remodeled several times to keep pace with increased use and new medical technology. Chuck Cecil Photo.

The first Brookings County Courthouse was built in 1983 at a cost of $7,000, of which the City of Brookings contributed $4,000. The remaining $3,000 was a county-wide levy. The new building measured 59x56 feet. It was sold at auction in 1912 to Lars Otterness for $620 when the current courthouse was completed on the same block. George Norby Photo.

The laying of the cornerstone for the present County Courthouse was held on May 10, 1911, and the renaissance revival building was completed the next year at a cost of $100,000. Planners were adamant that two restrooms for use by farmers and their wives when in Brookings be included in the floor plan. It also had a "vacuum cleaning system." George Norby Photo.

Finishing touches are underway for the courthouse in this photo taken in the fall of 1912. Note the car in front. Originally, a curved drive extended to the front door where the sidewalk is today. George Norby Photo.

The courthouse as it appears today. At right is a memorial garden honoring veterans of the various wars. Space in the building is at a premium and the county commissioners are exploring ways to free up space, such as computerizing old records. Chuck Cecil Photo.

72

As a bond sales leader during WW II, Brookings had the honor of having a troop transport ship named after it. The Victory ship was launched Nov. 27, 1944, at Wilmington, CA, and in 1986, it was towed to sea and used as a target ship until it sank. County Commission Photo.

Long before the SS Brookings took to the water, a crew of 16 installed water mains on a Brookings street. Janet Brandsma Photo.

A road grading crew heads north, smoothing the dirt and graveled Main Avenue near the intersection with Fourth Street. Interestingly, the workers wore white shirts and the man bringing up the rear is wearing a suit. Note the cleats on the steam traction engine, extending out from the iron wheels several inches, apparently for more grip. As always through the years, sidewalk engineers, at right, stand ready to give good, sound advice. Downtown Improvement, Doris Roden, Photo.

Chief J. J. Connelly, at left, and other city and county law enforcement officials in the 1920s, pose with the results of recent liquor raids which were part of the battles between moonshiners and the law during the Prohibition Years. The Ram, Tom and Gwen Yseth, Photo.

Chapter Six

Churches

First Lutheran Church at the north end of Main Avenue. Chuck Cecil Photo.

The new $6 million Catholic Church looking northwest. The church contains classrooms for an elementary school. Note the unusual roof line over the sanctuary at right, which is covered with copper sheeting. Chuck Cecil Photo.

The early Baptist Church. Brookings Public Library Photo.

The First Presbyterian Church. Note the gravel and dirt street, which is today's Fourth Street. But when this picture was taken, as the caption in white ink on the photo indicates, it was known as Williams Street. Street names were changed by city leaders in 1901 to numerical designations. The church today does not have the spires atop the railing around the tower, but otherwise is very similar. A white, steepled church of wood frame construction can be seen a block away from this church. Brookings Public Library Photo.

The United Presbyterian Church in the early years. Note the unusual round stained glass window, which is very much like the window in the First Methodist Church shown below. Brookings Public Library Photo.

A recent picture of the First United Methodist Church at 625 Fifth Street. Chuck Cecil Photo.

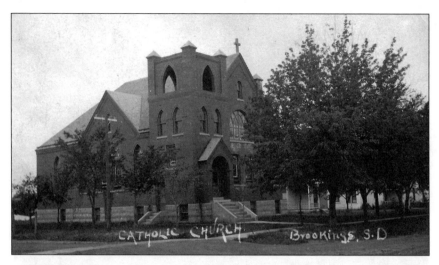

The old Catholic Church at Fourth Street and Medary, with its tower. Below, the same church after the tower was removed. George Norby Photos.

This is the First Methodist Church on Fifth Street looking west toward Main Avenue. Between 1901 and 1908, five churches were built in Brookings, including this one that was completed in 1904. The first new church building of the century, the Presbyterian Church, was built in 1901. This Methodist Church came next, followed by the Catholic Church on Medary Avenue and Fourth Street in 1906. Also built in 1906 was the United Presbyterian Church followed two years later by the Lutheran Church. Brookings Public Library Collection.

An early photograph of the Norwegian Lutheran Church that was built in 1908-09 at the corner of Seventh Street and North Main Avenue. It was the fifth new church built in Brookings during the first decade of the 20th century. In 1956, the present First Lutheran Church was constructed at the end of North Main Avenue. The old church a block south was torn down and an apartment house built in its place. Brookings Public Library Collection.

Chapter Seven

Parades and Celebrations

It was cause for celebration in Brookings when the smoke stack of the power plant came down in August 1982. Electrical power from the Missouri River dams was serving Brookings, and most businesses had converted from steam heat. The stack and power plant were located where the city parking lot is now, next to the Elks Club. George Norby Photo.

The 1920 Fourth of July on Main Avenue included a stage show at the Third Street intersection. The Montgomery Ward Building is at right. In addition to the flag in the foreground, notice others in the background. There is one flown from the top of the Montgomery Ward Building and two atop power poles on both sides of the street. The pole at left has also been wound with red, white and blue bunting. This intersection, because it was close to the busy Brookings House Hotel and the railroad depot, was the location of choice for celebrations. The stage show on the next page was held on another Fourth of July at the same location. George Norby Photo.

A block east of where the photo at top was taken, the 2000 Fourth of July parade passes the flag, different only in the number of stars it displays. In the background is the Brookings Public Library. Chuck Cecil Photo.

A daredevil performs during an early 1900s Fourth of July celebration. The stage show is being held at the intersection of Main Avenue and Third Street. Signs on the bottom of the stage remind spectators to buy carnival novelties at Irwin's Drug Store. George Norby Photo.

Students celebrating Hobo Day were as fun-loving then as they are now. In this photograph, a crowd of smiling onlookers gathers around a float, which is a horse-drawn buggy. A student is standing before a seated professor in the buggy, probably responding to an academic question posed by the professor. Another student holds a long bamboo fishing pole for a reason now unknown. George Norby Photo.

This bummobile, christened "Souped Up Chevy" by its builders, haltingly heads south down Main Avenue between Fifth and Fourth Streets in a late 1950s Hobo Day parade. For safety reasons, bummobiles were discouraged from entering the parade in the 1970s. George Norby Photo.

Shoppers search for bargains during a three-day Crazy Days promotion on Main Avenue in the early 1960s. This bargain table of specials is set up in front of the Sears Store. George Norby Photo.

While mothers shopped for Crazy Days specials, kids were treated to free rides sponsored by Brookings automobile dealers. This picture looks southeast toward the Montgomery Ward Building. George Norby Photo.

WW I soldiers marching north on Main Avenue, probably in the late teens or early 1920s. George Norby Photo.

Veterans march south on Main in this 1910 parade. George Norby Photo.

Brookings' first band, known far and wide as the Cornet Band, was popular at county parades and celebrations. The drummer at left is S. W. Lockwood. Then Gene Parker, Frank Adams and Ole Knutson. The tall baritone player second from right is Grant Davis. George Norby Photo.

Beauties and beasts in Brookings

A 1950s Hobo Day float is propelled by students underneath pushing and steering it past the five and dime store, which is Rude's Furniture Store today. A "stunt car," now known as a bummobile, follows. SDSU Photo.

When the circus came to Brookings, the parade whetted the appetites of the young and old. Here caged lions contentedly watch the world go by as a decorative wagon pulled by a span of matching white horses progresses north on Main Avenue in 1905. The sign on the store behind the wagon advertises a "Sacrifice Sale" of dry goods and clothing. The smaller sign says: "Bicycles Checked." George Norby Photo.

A makeshift band rides on this horsedrawn, decorated float in a Hobo Day parade in about 1918. It is passing by the Montgomery Ward Building in the background. Ed Fuller Photo.

SDSC coeds march single file in the Hobo Day parade in about 1918. Then, every college student joined in the parade, marching single file close to the sidewalk, then making a turn at the south end of Main Avenue and marching back north. Note the buttoned shoes the girls are wearing. Ed Fuller photo.

Chapter Eight

School Days

Armed with her juggling or exercise clubs, this Brookings student celebrates her accomplishments at school by posing proudly at Oyloe Studios. Brookings County Histrorical Society Photo.

This old building on the corner of Fourth Street and Fifth Avenue was the city's first school. When this photo was taken about the turn of the century, it was the home of the *Brookings Register*. It was built for $2,000 and completed April 15, 1880. George Norby Photo.

The beautiful old school known as the Red Castle was built at a cost of $10,000 in August 1888. It was located about where the Central Elementary School is now located. The building was torn down in 1935. A portion of the window lintel on the first floor window at right, in the form of the head of a Native American, was saved and is on display at the Brookings County Historical Society Museum in Volga. George Norby Photo.

With a continued rapid growth in school-age children in Brookings, this new primary school building was constructed in 1908. It was located where the old middle school gymnasium is now. George Norby Photo.

Brookings junior and senior high school students gathered for this group picture, probably in the early 1920s. Chances are the picture was taken in the recently completed new High School built in 1921. George Norby Photo.

One of the best bargains for Brookings taxpayers was the building of this school to house junior high school students. It is now Central Elementary on Fourth Street near the Courthouse Square. It is on the site of the old Red Castle School and was built during the 1930s as a WPA project for just $90,000. Chuck Cecil Photo.

The old, abandoned high school is now known as the 1921 Building. That was the year it was built at a cost of $165,000. It was dedicated March 4, 1937. Dr. C. W. Pugsley, president of SDSC, was the speaker. The building was considered one of the best designed in the state, built for an enrollment of 650. Interestingly, bonded funds to pay for the building were short of actual costs so the second floor was left unfinished for a few years until the school board funded that section. The building was later used as the Middle School, then sold to the county. At one time, county commissioners wanted to use it for additional courthouse office space, but that was abandoned. It is now being considered as a business office site by private contractors. Chuck Cecil Photo.

Hillcrest Elementary School was opened in 1954 at Fifteenth Avenue and Third Street. It was built at a cost of $225,000. Originally designed for grades one through six, by the time it was built the enrollment had grown so that space was limited to just kindergarten through third grade. Over the years it has been remodeled and expanded many, many times. Chuck Cecil Photo.

The current high school was opened in 1967 at a cost of $2.14 million. It, too, has been remodeled to keep pace with needs. A major addition was being discussed by the school board in 2003. Chuck Cecil Photo.

The newest addition to the city's school system is the $11.8 million George S. Mickelson Middle School, named to honor the memory of the former Brookings resident who was killed in an airplane crash in 1993 while serving as governor. Chuck Cecil Photo.

Chapter Nine

Transportation

This 1990s aerial of Brookings clearly shows the city's excellent transportation infrastructure, from the Brookings Airport at left center, to Highway 14 at the top and its bypass angling out from West Brookings, to the Dakota, Minnesota and Eastern (DM&E) railroad line through the center of town. EROS photo.

The A. B. Allisons outside their home at Third Street and Sixth Avenue where the Public Library now stands. Brookings Public Library Photo.

In 1910, Jim Natesta, an early Medary Village and Brookings merchant, and Hal Morehouse set out to drive this Buick from Brookings to Los Angeles, CA, the first Buick to ever make the trip. Netasta is at the wheel as they leave from in front of the First National Bank. Note knobby rear wheels and smooth front wheels. No details are available about the trip, or if they ever made it to California. Brookings Public Library Photo.

Touring cars were probably available at the A. B. Allison Land Agency to take new arrivals out to inspect farm land for sale. The office was at the northwest corner of Third Street and Main Avenue. Note the signs painted on the side of the building, including reference to "Wild Lands." Brookings Public Library Photo.

Most of the cars parked on Main Avenue between Fourth and Third Streets were canvas-topped and open-sided in the 1920s, when this photograph looking north was taken. One of the first automobiles in Brookings was a one-cylinder Cadillac Model A owned by Engineering Professor Halvor Solberg. One tire for his machine, 3x28, cost $27 and had a life of about 3,000 miles. Top speed for Prof. Solberg's car was 15 miles an hour. George Norby Photo.

One of several North Western trains steams through Brookings on a cold winter's day in the early 1950s. Much of the commerce of Brookings evolved around the daily arrival and departure of the trains. At times, over a dozen trains passed through town each day. As the least expensive mode of transportation for lengthy trips, college athletic teams, music groups and others rode trains to far off destinations or home for the holidays. George Norby Photo.

Depot Agent Howard Graham, right, served this community and the North Western Railroad for 17 years, retiring in 1952 after 40 years of railroading. Bob Severance is at left. Above his typewriter is the depot's telegraph receiver. Shirley Lyons Photo.

Old veterans were among those gathered at the depot in 1916 to see troops off for duty during WW I. George Norby Photo.

The streamlined Dakota 400 speeds across the Main Avenue crossing in the early 1950s. George Norby Photo.

Brookings Main Avenue traffic in the 1920s, looking north. George Norby Photo.

This 2000 photo of the Paula Motors complex looks northeast toward Wal-Mart and the now closed K-Mart in east Brookings. In the 1950s, Brookings had over a dozen car dealers, most located in or near the downtown district. By the turn of the century, there were just two new car dealerships remaining, both located far from Main Avenue. Chuck Cecil Photo.

The lone reminder today of the city's first airport is this shell of a hangar on the lowlands in south Brookings. Unfortunately, the grass runway of the first airport tended to attract flood waters, some of which can be seen at left. Later in the building's life it was a beer hall, but it failed in that assignment, too. Jim Talbert Photo.

Western Airlines initiated the first air service to Brookings on June 1, 1950, with ceremonies featuring Mayor Homer Dwiggins and Governor George T. Mickelson. Over 2,000 residents attended the event and watched as the first east-bound Brookings air passenger, Joe Oines of Oines Motor Co., boarded this DC-3 and left for a quick trip to Minneapolis. The DC-3 was the WWII Dakota that carried paratroopers for the airborne drop over Normandy on D-Day. George Norby Photo.

To meet the traffic needs of a growing Brookings that was expanding to the south, the city in the 1980s completed this broad, four-lane roadway extension to Main Avenue. This aerial photo looks north toward downtown Brookings. Chuck Cecil Photo.

Chapter Ten

Cars and Drive-Ins

President Calvin Coolidge, his son John and wife Grace, after arriving by special train at the Brookings Depot on Sept. 10, 1927, in the presidential car. They were preparing for the drive to the campus where he dedicated Lincoln Memorial Library and nearby Coolidge Sylvan Theater. SDSU Photo.

The Dybdahl Motor Company across the street north of the First National Bank on Fifth Street is now the bank's office building. Ivar Dybdahl started the business in 1915 and his son and daughter, Irwin and Dora, continued after their father retired. They closed Dybdahl Motor Company in the early 1970s. George Norby Photo.

Among the used cars for sale at Kellogg's Used Cars in 1958 was this classy 1955 Studebaker Commander. The car lot was at 303 Third Street. George Norby Photo.

Ron Einspahr bought the Ford, Mercury and Lincoln dealership in Brookings in 1968. It was then located on Fifth Street a block west of the Post Office. The gas company building was built on the lot. Einspahr later moved into new facilities on Eighth Street South. George Norby Photo.

A July Fourth parade on Main Avenue. The cars are making a U-turn near the railroad crossing. By 1915, there were 975 cars registered in the county. At the beginning of the 1920s, the number had grown to 1,173. At decade's end, there were 4,838 cars registered in the county. Note the non-traditional placement of the steering wheels on the left side. Brookings County Historical Society Photo.

The Jackrabbit station operated for decades on Medary a block south of the Campanile on campus. Then all "filling stations" provided full services, including pumping the gas, cleaning the windows, and checking fluids. If you asked, they would also empty your ashtray. This photo was taken in 1955. George Norby Photo.

Sturdevant's "mascot" for many years was this 1916 Saxon, proudly shown here by Vance Janssen, left, and owner Clarence Sturdevant. The business was where the Aho Law Office is today, north of the Post Office. George Norby Photo.

The Corral was Brookings' first drive-in at 1816 Sixth Street. The burro painted on the side of the building was the object of vandals who enjoyed painting extra "embellishments." When the Dairy Queen opened in 1950, the Corral introduced the "Dairy Sno" to compete. Note the gravel surface, considered ideal for "wheelies" by the town's young "hot rod" showoffs. George Norby Photo.

The Dairy Queen opened in 1950 and continued for nearly 50 years until razed to make room for a quick stop gas and snack store on west Sixth Street. Dairy Queen currently operates on 22nd Avenue. George Norby Photo.

The A&W introduced a new wrinkle in drive-ins in Brookings in this covered parking area. The Corral was located nearby. George Norby Photo.

The A&W introduced a foot-long hotdog to Brookings in the mid-1950s, and to promote the innovation, owner Ed McComish cooked one up for advertising purposes that was a little longer than 12 inches. Note that a root beer was five cents for a mug-full. George Norby Photo.

The Zesto is still doing business at the same spot it has always occupied, across from the swimming pool. The trees at right have been cut down and McDonald's Golden Arch has taken root. Note the hungry hound picking up the leftovers. George Norby Photo.

The Purple Cow on south Main Avenue. As the poem says, "I've never seen a purple cow and I never hope to see one. But I can tell you here and now, I'd rather see than be one." It's now The Barrel Drive-In. George Norby Photo.

Chapter Eleven

Signs Of The Times

The lack of a proper rest room, especially for the ladies, was remedied if only for this early Hobo Day parade. The sign advertises "Ladies Restroom, Half Block." George Norby Photo.

When the courthouse was being planned, commissioners insisted on rest rooms for visiting farm families to use. But it wasn't until 1953 that the city constructed this lounge on Fourth Street. Note the creative use of the apostrophe. George Norby Photo.

For years Brookings men bought their tobacco products and magazines at Logue's Corner. A block away, smoke of another kind spewed out of the city's coal-fired power plant, below, behind Bozied's Produce Company on Third Street. George Norby Photos.

Jerry Lewis was starring in the 1958 State Theater show, "Don't Give Up The Ship." In 1964, a new marquee and modern decorative panels, below, dressed up the building where Richard Boone was on the screen. The temporary United Charities thermometer had a 1964 goal of $15,000. George Norby Photo.

Brookings Cafe
Menu a la carte

Cold Meats

Assorted Meats	50	Roast Pork	50
Chicken	50	Boiled Ham	50
Roast Beef	50	Boiled Beef Tongue	50

Potato Salad served with Cold Meats

Sandwiches

Boiled Ham	10	Club	40
Fried Ham	15	Egg	15
Cheese	15	Roast Pork	15
Hamberger	15	Roast Beef	15
Chicken	20	Beef Tongue	15
Ham and Egg	20	Sardines	15
Denver	25		

Salads

Potato	15	Shrimp	40
Lobster	40	Tomato	15
Chicken	35	Salmon	35
Combination	25	Cucumber	15
Lettuce	10		

Vegetables

French Fried Potatoes	15	American Fried Potatoes	10
Hash Brown Potatoes	15	Lyonnaise	15
Stewed Peas	15	Tomatoes	15
Stewed Corn	15	Spinach	15
String Beans	15	Asparagus on Toast	30

Cakes, Toast and Cereals

Wheat Cakes	20	French Toast	30
Rolls	10	Oatmeal with Cream	20
Doughnuts	5	Grape Nuts with Cream	20
Dry Toast	10	Corn Flakes with Cream	20
Buttered Toast	10	Shredded Wheat Biscuit,	
Milk Toast	20	with Cream	20
Cream Toast	30		

Fruit and Preserves

Apple Sauce	10	Sliced Oranges	15
Sliced Bananas, with Cream	20	Half Grape Fruit	15

Drinks

Coffee	5	Chocolate	10
Tea	5	Cocoa	10
Milk	5	Cream, per glass	10

If We Please You, Tell Others; If Not, Tell Us

Not Responsible for Personal Property

REGISTER PUBLISHING COMPANY

At the Brookings Cafe in the 1930s, you could buy milk toast for 20 cents and a beef tongue sandwich for a nickel less. Many of these items, not surprisingly, no longer appear on cafe menus.
Brookings County Historical Society.

The art deco College Theater opened Jan. 5, 1942. In February 1954, CinemaScope came to town for the first time with the showing of "The Robe." The last picture show at the College was "Blazing Saddles" on May 6, 1976. At that time, KBRK studios were upstairs. Mike's Eat Shoppe, a popular eating spot at left, had closed. In the 1950s, it was not unusual to have lines of prospective diners filling the sidewalk at left and lines of movie goers waiting to buy tickets bending out to the right. Below, the opening date of the Sioux Drive-In Theater south of town was always difficult to predict, for obvious reasons. George Norby Photos.

In the 1950s, pork chops were 59 cents a pound and rubber jar seals for canning sold three for a quarter at the National Tea grocery store on Fifth Street, west of Nick's Hamburger Shop. At that time, a lunch counter was located in the front of the store and attracted a large noon-time college crowd. The building stood empty for a number of years, and in the late 1970s the *Brookings Register* remodeled and moved in. George Norby Photo.

The first 24-hour, seven-day-a-week grocery store arrived in town in the 1950s. Spies Super Valu was on Sixth Street between Fifth and Sixth Avenue. The building is now home of the Graham Tire Company. George Norby Photo.

Bob and Lorne Bartling in 1964 with an antique advertising sign their father, Earl H. Bartling and partner George Sellers placed at farmsteads in the area shortly after starting the business in 1918. Below, Chan Shirley and Gerritt Heida try selling out the back door at Shirley Pharmacy across Main Avenue from Bartlings. George Norby Photo.

Chapter Twelve

Sports and Recreation

Joe Thorne, a star fullback and all-conference player for the Jackrabbits in 1959, 1960, and 1961, with Ralph Ginn, head football coach. After graduation, Thorne served in the Army as a helicopter pilot in Vietnam. He was killed in action on Easter Sunday, April 19, 1965. Ginn retired from coaching and was was successful running for Commissioner of Schools and Public Lands. SDSU Photo.

A family picnic and fishing trip at Lake Campbell. Lashed to the posts of the surrey are several fish, which appear to be bullheads. There are only two bamboo fishing poles displayed, which might imply that most of the people shown came along for the ride and the picnic. Brookings Public Library Photo.

The only SDSU athlete ever to be drafted into two professional sports is Ed Maras, class of 1966. Green Bay liked his football talents and the Baltimore Orioles his pitching. In the days when just one collegiate All-American team was selected, Maras made the first nine as a first baseman, along with Arizona State outfielder Reggie Jackson. From Windom, MN, Maras, 6'2" and 225 pounds, led the Rabbits to a conference baseball championship his junior year, batting .391. He is a member of the Jackrabbit Hall of Fame. SDSU Photos.

This fieldstone entrance to Pioneer Park was constructed in 1929 on the city's 40th anniversary. The bandshell, which is still in use, was a federal project in 1936 during the Depression. It was designed by the son of SDSC President C. W. Pugsley and built with WPA funds. The park is the former site of the city's first fairgrounds, shown below. George Norby Photo.

To attract tourists, the city built these small log cabins and operated a tourist camp about a block east of the present swimming pool. The camp covered eight acres and had a store, hot showers, electric lights, and regular city police patrols.

Farmers parade their best work horses by the Fairgrounds stands, at right, and the judges stand, at left, in 1910. Note the large stock pavilion at left. It was about where the park entry above is located. Brookings County Historical Society Photo.

119

The Brookings County Stock Pavilion in the early 1900s was part of a huge fairgrounds about where Pioneer Park is located today along Sixth Street. It was the most modern of the day and even included heated bleachers accomplished by an ingenious system of hot water pipes placed under the seats. Brookings County Historical Society Photo.

About 100 years after the building at the top of the page was built, at the other end of town, this state-of-the-art multi-purpose building went up in the late 1990s, financed mostly by taxes from the city and the county. The cost was about $12 or $13 million. In 2003, the name of the facility was changed from Brookings MultiPlex to the Swiftel Center after naming rights were sold to the city-owned telephone company for $50,000. The county extension offices are located in the section at right. The pavilion is suitable for everything from elaborate stage shows and concerts to rodeos, wrestling matches, and basketball games. Chuck Cecil Photo.

Danceland on the east shore of Lake Campbell started out in the 1920s prohibition days as a rooming house for visting out-of-state pheasant hunters. It expanded over the years, and in the 1930s and into the 1980s it was a popular eating and dancing stop. These pictures were taken in the 1930s. Later, the west wall (at left in the photo above), was removed and an addition built to accommodate booths. In 1986 when it was owned by Butch Oseby, it was destroyed by fire in a Christmas Eve blaze. After the lot was cleared of debris, a new owner placed a smaller building on the site and opened a pub and cafe. George Norby Photo.

For games in the old Barn at SDSU, fans (some with coffee pots) started lining up at noon on game day in the mid-1950s. The clock facsimile says it's 2:45 p.m., and another sign says that the doors open at 5:30 p.m. Just 450 general admission tickets were available for the SDSU-USD game. Below, in the new Frost Arena on opening night, Feb. 24, 1973, 8,000 fans watched SDSU defeat Augustana 84-76. The record Frost Arena crowd was 9,456 set on Feb. 11, 1989, when SDSU downed Augustana 90-77.

Chuck Cecil Photos.

After decades of often contentious discussions about the location of the city's swimming pool, it was finally built in east Brookings rather than west Brookings at Pioneer Park. Costing just $33,000, which included $8,000 in WPA funds, the pool opened Aug. 23, 1937. In May 1982, a pool addition costing $870,000 was approved. In this 1950s photo, note the motel cabins in the background. The Hillside Motel has since been sold and the land will be used for a water slide. George Norby Photo.

Coughlin-Alumni Stadium welcomed its first game in 1962. It was built with donated funds. In 2002, the University and the Brookings School system reached an agreement for the high school to play its games at the stadium. Lights were installed by the school district. The first ever night game at the stadium was on Aug. 25, 2002, when the Bobcats played Yankton. SDSU Photo.

Chapter Thirteen

Then and Now

The Grand Army of the Republic (GAR) organization in Brookings constructed a meeting hall in 1984-85 at 311 Fifth Street, top left. It was later
moved to 126 Medary Avenue and used as the Odd Fellows Hall, top right.
In 2000 it was torn down and a new building for storage and business was
constructed on the site by Lyle Prussman's Odd Fellows Rentals, bottom
photo. George Norby Photo, top left, and Chuck Cecil Photos.

What was the Arctic Drive-In in the 1980s is now Mr. Movies at 621 Sixth Street. Chuck Cecil Photos.

What in the 1950s was Robertson Auto Electric at 411 Fourth Street is now Threads of Memories, an antique store. At far right is a portion of the Swiftel Communications office, the new name of the Brookings telephone department. George Norby Photo and Chuck Cecil Photo.

The Purple Cow at Main Avenue and Eighth Street South is now the Barrel Drive-In. Note small speaker on the post at left used for placing orders from your car. As the sign says, there were no car hops and "no tips." George Norby Photo and Chuck Cecil Photo.

What was once the jail as well as the home of the Brookings County Sheriff has been replaced with a more spacious building. The old jail was not designed with security or prisoner comfort in mind. Stories are told of friends of the incarcerated driving up near a cell window at this building and passing a rubber hose to the occupant so that he could suck up beer or some other liquid that was hidden in the car of the visitor. In the 1920s, a notorious local bootlegger, given trustee status, often crawled out the upper floor window to join in parties held about town. A surprised sheriff on a late-night raid discovered his trustee with a drink in his hand. George Norby Photo and Chuck Cecil Photo.

The second White Spot on west Sixth Street in the 1950s, where first Lawrence Dyball and then Leonard Sanders operated the tiny restaurant. The original White Spot was started about 100 yards to the west by automobile dealer Forrest Frie. His White Spot first opened in 1948 at 410 West Sixth Street. The address is no more since the Highway 14 bypass was constructed at that location. Sandy's White Spot operated until the 1970s when the building was purchased and became a pet-grooming business owned by Terry Robuck. Before that, it was a vacuum cleaner repair shop and a bait shop. The pre-fabricated building is said to be a collector's item now. For the 2002 Brookings Car Festival held in Pioneer Park opposite the White Spot, the old building was selected as the festival logo. George Norby Photo.

Chuck Cecil Photo.

130

Fire of unknown origin broke out in Ione's Cafe at 423 Main Avenue during the cold night of March 3, 1985. LeRoy VanderPool, 66, who lived upstairs, died in the blaze. Also destroyed were a gift shop and optometric office at 425 Main. The site is now an empty lot, shown below. Nick's Hamburger Shop is at far right. George Norby Photos.

After a night on the town in the 1950s, The Pheasant Cafe was the place to go for a midnight snack. The north end was a filling station. Ray Gile bought the business, started in 1949, from Carl Grossman late in the 1950s. He took down the pheasant sign and renamed the place. In 1966, Ron Olson operated the business and gave it back its name. The Pheasant was granted a liquor license in 1968. Olson soon closed the car service and expanded the restaurant and lounge. He completely remodeled the building in the 1990s. The old pheasant sign stored behind the business deteriorated and was finally junked. Olson completed 37 years as owner in 2003. Ron Olson, George Norby and Chuck Cecil Photos.

This was the 1950s home of Marshall Produce and Wayne Feeds at 215 Fifth Avenue, next to Harold's Printing, now owned by Pat Leary. The produce house is now an attractive office building. Note the concrete post street marker at right, one of hundreds that have since been replaced with more snowplow friendly street signs. George Norby Photo.

Not only has the old Medary Standard Service Station from the 1950s changed, but Sixth Street is in much better repair. When the photo above was taken, gas was advertised at 30 cents a gallon, as the makeshift sign at the entrance suggests. Perhaps a gas war was underway at the time. By 2003, new owner Tom Bozied had not only built a new, modern facility, but the old residential home at right was gone. The three-story apartment building at left, set at an angle facing the Medary and Sixth Street intersection, remains today. Note the curbside grass by the sign in the photo at top. George Norby Photo.

Chuck Cecil Photo.

The fire hall in the old City Hall building on Fourth Street was too small to handle the requirements of a growing city for fire protection. In 1962, the old Bates Hotel at the Third Street and Third Avenue intesection was purchased by the city and a new fire hall took shape, with the finished product shown below. That's the former LeFevre Motor Company building in the background at right. The former Dudley Hotel, which became the Sawnee Hotel in 1937, is seen at left. A second fire hall was built in the 1980s on East Sixth Street, which is also the administrative office of the full-time fire chief, who works with over 40 volunteer fire fighters. George Norby Photo.

Chuck Cecil Photo.

The Rainbow Cafe, 407 Main Avenue, next to the Sears Store and a five & dime store, now Rude's Furniture Store, was a popular restaurant during the late 1940s and early 1950s. For a while, it was Wong's Cafe. It was then extensively remodeled and re-named Mac's in the 1980s, but a fire destroyed the business soon after it opened and the empty lot is now fronted with a plywood fence, seen at left. It is the second empty lot in the 400 block of Main Avenue. George Norby Photo.

Chuck Cecil Photo.

In the 1940s, '50s, and '60s, this was as close to a twenty-first century strip mall as it got. The Cottage Store, on Medary Avenue one-half block from the Campanile, did a good business with a steady stream of college students stopping by for a sack of groceries. The small barber shop owned by Hugo Mock, and then Jack McClemens, at left, was also a popular spot. A small cafe operated in the south portion of the building, at right. It served the largest pancakes in town. Note the old lamp post, and near it a sign which advertised the day's Cottage and cafe specials. Today, the building is gone, as well as residential homes on either side of it, and the land has been purchased by the state. Below, the Pugsley Student Center built in 1940 is now university office space. The Student Book Store was located on the bottom floor of the wing at left near the Public Television satellite dishes. George Norby Photo.

Chuck Cecil Photo.

137

In the 1950s on Sixth Street west of Main Avenue, Milfs Body Shop and a huge elm dominated the scene. The elm was a victim of Dutch Elm disease in the 1970s, but while in its prime, Mr. Milfs surely qualified as an honest-to-goodness shade tree mechanic. West of Milfs was a small high school hang-out in the 1950s, an ice cream shop which was operated by elementary teacher Francis (Franny) Dolan. The shop was the former Sykes Cafe. The property is now the offices for Moriarty Rentals and other stores. Interestingly, another large elm tree down the street (see below) still survives. George Norby Photo.

Chuck Cecil Photo.

In 1955, Naiem Bozied opened his Conoco Station at the southeast intersection of Sixth Street and Main Avenue. He operated it until 1980 when he sold it and hauled away some of his memorabilia from 25 years in business, at right. From the first day, Bozied offered 24-hour service until 1973 when a national gas shortage mandated an earlier closing time. Donna Burns photos.

The Conoco Station above was remodeled and refurbished by BANKFIRST, owned by former Brookings resident and Brookings High School and 1959 South Dakota State University graduate Mert Lund. He purchased the bank in Toronto, SD, in 1972 and added this bank and others in Sioux Falls, Chandler, AZ, and Minneapolis, plus credit card services. BANKFIRST has over $900 million in assets and about 1,000 employees. In 2003, this bank moved to another location on 22nd Avenue. The gas pumps became the location of the drive-up service window, bottom photo. Chuck Cecil Photo.

Brookings Mayors

Scott Munsterman
2003-

Virgil Herriott
1999-2003

Wayne Hauschild
1993-1999

Orrin Juel
1970-1980 &1990-1993

Gail Robertson
1985-1990

Roger Prunty
1980-1985

Forrest G. Frie
1964-1970

Oliver Gottschalk
1960-1962

Homer Dwiggins
1939-1952; 1954-1960;
1962-1964

1881-R. S. Hadley	1903-05-John C. Jenkins
1882-83-A. A. Aiken	1905-07-Frank M. Kerner
1883-84-G. A. Mathews	1907-09-H. B. Mathews
1885-87-H. H. Natwick	1909-13-W. H. Leighty
1887-89-G. A. Mathews	1913-15-C. A. Johnson
1890-91-W. H. Roddle	1915-17-H. B. Mathews
1891-John F. Diamond	1917-20-W. H. Leighty
1891-94-G. J. Coller	1920-25-T. I. Flittie
1894-95-Philo Hall	1925-1930-C. O. Trygstad
1895-97-A. W. Hyde	1930-35-I. B. Johnson
1897-1903-G. A. Mathews	1935-39-Charles Gauken

This rare photo looking west was taken on Oct. 31, 1901, from the roof of the college's Solberg Hall. Placement of yet-to-be-built Lincoln Library, Sylvan Theater, and the Campanile are marked, as is the future location of Pugsley along Ninth Street. Eleventh Avenue heads left off Ninth Street at left. Ninth Street (now Harvey Dunn Street) continues at top right, but later would be rebuilt a block to the left. Ninth would become Harvey Dunn (Tenth) Street. The printed notation is about where the old City Hospital, now West Hall, is located. Woodbine Cottage can be seen at far right. The campus is on a slight rise and townspeople referred to the college as being "up on the hill." The left half of this photo is printed on the next page. Ed Fuller Photo.

11th Ave.

This is the second half of the photo which shows the campus as it appeared on Oct. 31, 1901. The picture, looking to the southwest, was taken from the roof of Solberg Hall on the SDSU campus. The dirt street at lower right is Ninth Street and the road running from right toward the center of the picture is Eleventh Avenue going south. Medary is the street barely visible at upper right. Crothers Engineering Hall is now located where the house in the foreground at right is. If there was a Twelfth Avenue at that time, it would be just behind the home's outbuildings at left. A water tower can be seen on the horizon above the house, and just to the right of the tower are taller buildings, probably the Red Castle School House among them, and some or all of the six grain elevators the city had at that time. Twenty years before this photo was taken, Brookings was incorporated as a city. A month before this October photo was taken, the first passenger train to Redfield left the Brookings depot. Ed Fuller Photo.

Aerial view of downtown Brookings, looking northeast, 1956